Best-Ever Chicken Recipes

by Christine Koury

BARRON'S

New York · London · Toronto · Sydney

All inquiries should be addressed to:

Barron's Educational Series, Inc.
250 Wireless Boulevard
Hauppauge, New York 11788

International Standard Book
No. 0-8120-5629-9
Library of Congress Catalog Card
No. 84-24220

**Library of Congress Cataloging in
Publication Data**
Koury, Christine.
  Best-ever chicken recipes.

  Includes index.
  1. Cookery (Chicken) 1. Title.
TX750.K68 1985 641.6'65 84-24220
ISBN 0-8120-5629-9
PRINTED IN HONG KONG
7 8 9 490 9 8 7 6 5 4 3 2

Credits

Photography
Color photographs: Matthew Klein
Food stylist: Andrea Swenson
Stylist: Linda Cheverton

Author Christine Koury is food editor at
  Woman's World magazine. She is also
  the author of another Easy Cooking
  book, *Great Desserts.*

Cover and book design: Milton Glaser, Inc.

INTRODUCTION

Lending itself to many different ways of cooking—roasting and broiling, sautéing and frying, boiling and barbecuing—chicken is a versatile food, with a flavor assertive enough to be eaten plain yet delicate enough to be enhanced by the addition of sauces, gravies, and any number of other ingredients. Simple enough for an everyday dinner, chicken can be dressed up for elegant company fare, and it's equally popular hot and cold.

Chicken is nutritious. Not only is it an excellent source of protein, providing as much as red meats, it is lower in fat and calories than such meats as beef and pork. Economically speaking, too, chicken is a nutritional bargain that's hard to beat—it's lower in cost per edible pound of protein than meat.

TYPES OF CHICKEN

The younger the chicken, the more tender it will be. The age of the bird should be considered when deciding the cooking method.

BROILER-FRYERS   May also be found labeled as frying chickens or broilers. These birds, 7 to 9 weeks old, weighing 1½ to 4 pounds, are really the all-purpose chicken. Because they are young, they are tender, and do not need as long a cooking time as older birds of the same weight. They are suitable for roasting whole, stuffed or unstuffed, and can be baked, broiled, fried, barbecued, or simmered, either whole or in pieces.

ROASTING CHICKENS   Older and larger than broiler-fryers, these weigh between 3½ to 6 pounds and are about 16 weeks old. They are excellent for frying and barbecuing, as well as for roasting.

STEWING HENS OR FOWL   These mature hens weigh between 3 to 5 pounds, and are less tender and have more fat than younger birds. They require slow, moist cooking and are particularly good for stewing. They make a very flavorful stock, and they work well in dishes that call for cooked chicken such as creamed chicken and pot pie.

CAPONS   Under 7 months old, these are desexed male birds that weigh 4 to 7 pounds. Excellent for roasting, they have good flavor and contain a good deal of white meat.

PURCHASING

Almost all chicken is sold ready to cook, and it comes in a wide variety of ways—whole, halved, quartered, or cut up into serving pieces; in packages of breasts (whole, split, or boned); legs, drumsticks, thighs, or wings.

If cost is a factor, remember that buying chicken in parts is more expensive than buying the whole bird, breasts being the most expensive because they are the meatiest part of the bird. To be economical, buy a whole chicken and cut it into quarters or pieces yourself. And remember that larger chickens are a better buy because they contain a higher percentage of meat to bone (a whole chicken yields about half its purchased weight in edible cooked meat).

Before chickens are sent to the market, they are chilled quickly, then stored at 28 to 32 degrees. This increases their shelf life and prevents bacteria from growing. Because of the low storage temperature, ice may form on the birds. Note that while the chicken you purchase may be partially frozen, it is still considered fresh. Such birds should be refrigerated and cooked as fresh, or frozen.

When buying a chicken, make sure it is properly chilled. Food-poisoning bacteria do not multiply rapidly in cold poultry. Also, check labels for dates. The date on the package is usually the last day the store should sell the poultry; do not buy any products that are not fresh. Look for high-quality chickens. A well-shaped body is a sign of meatiness; the skin should not have any discoloration or bruises and should be clean, and it should be healthy looking, not dingy, pale, or grayish. (The color of the skin itself is not a sign of quality, tenderness, flavor, nutritional value, or anything else; it is a reflection of what the bird was fed, and can vary from white to deep yellow.)

Never buy poultry with an off odor. If you discover a strong odor when you open the package, return the chicken to the store where you purchased it.

STORING

After you get home from the store, remove the wrapper from the chicken. Chickens usually come accompanied by their hearts, gizzards, livers, and necks; take these and the loose fat out of the body cavity. Wrap the chicken loosely in waxed paper, leaving the ends of the paper open so that air may circulate freely; fresh poultry should not be tightly wrapped when refrigerated. Refrigerate immediately, in the coldest part of the refrigerator (chicken should be stored at 40 degrees or below).

Since it is difficult to tell how long poultry can be kept before it spoils, chicken should be used 1 to 3 days after purchasing. If you don't plan to cook and serve the chicken within a couple of days, it is best to freeze it. Be sure to wrap the chicken properly, in freezer paper. Package pieces in sizes to fit your needs; label with date, names and number of parts, and weight. Place in a freezer set at 0 degrees. Poultry will keep for about 1 year in the freezer; longer storage may result in a loss of quality, but there should be no danger if the bird is eaten, as long as it was stored properly.

It is best and safest to thaw chicken in the refrigerator. A 4-pound bird will thaw in 1 to 1½ days in the refrigerator; a bird that weighs less can thaw in 12 to 16 hours. If it is absolutely necessary to thaw it quickly, place the chicken in an airtight wrapper and thaw in cold water; make sure the water covers the chicken, and change it frequently. Chicken that has been thawed should be used right away and should not be refrozen, which will result in a lowering of quality. *Never* stuff a chicken and then freeze or refrigerate it.

To store cooked poultry, do not let it stand longer than about 1½ hours at room temperature after cooking. Any leftovers should be refrigerated right after the meal is finished. Whole cooked chicken may be refrigerated for up to 3 days; pieces should be stored in the refrigerator only 2 days. Always remove any remaining stuffing from the bird and refrigerate it separately; gravy should also be stored separately. To keep fresh, wrap the chicken tightly in waxed paper or plastic wrap. If chicken has been cooked for use in a recipe that calls for already cooked chicken (such as salad), it should be refrigerated within half an hour after cooking.

PREPARATION AND COOKING

To prepare a bird, whole or cut up, for cooking, after the giblets and loose fat have been removed, wash the bird thoroughly (inside and out, if whole, and on all sides, if cut up), making sure it is completely cleaned of any organs that may have been left attached to the backbone.

If the chicken was frozen, thoroughly defrost it before you cook it; otherwise, it will cook unevenly. Once defrosted, use the chicken as you would a fresh one, within 2 days. If you cut up your own whole bird, it can be quartered or cut into 8 or 9 serving pieces—drumsticks, thighs, breast halves, and wings.

Chicken, at least in the Western world, is always cooked to the well-done stage. Use times only as a guide. To test if it is cooked, press the fleshy part of the thigh with a finger (protected with a paper towel); if the meat feels soft, it's cooked. On a whole bird, the leg should move up and down easily and the hip joint twist readily. The juices that come from the bird when it is pierced with a fork should be clear; if they are pink, the chicken needs to be cooked longer. A thermometer is an ideal way to tell if roast chicken is cooked. When it registers 180 to 185 degrees, the bird is done. If you are in doubt about whether or not the chicken is fully cooked, cut a slit down to the bone. If the meat is pink, it needs further cooking.

When a recipe calls for cooked chicken and you don't have leftover chicken to use, an ideal way to cook the chicken for use in the recipe is poaching.

To poach: place chicken pieces in a single layer in a large pot or skillet. Add water to cover. Cover and simmer 30 to 35 minutes, or until tender and juices run clear when chicken is pierced. The liquid is stock (or broth) and should be saved for gravies, sauces, or cooking vegetables.

YIELDS

WHOLE CHICKEN   Allow 8 to 12 ounces of uncooked chicken per serving; a 3-pound chicken yields 4 servings. One serving equals one-half breast or a thigh and drumstick, or a combination of smaller pieces.

BREASTS   Boned breasts, sometimes labeled as cutlets, are 100 percent meat. Allow one-half bone-in breast or 4 ounces boneless breast per serving.

THIGHS   Dark meat parts weighing about 4 ounces each. Allow two per serving.

DRUMSTICKS   Dark meat weighing 4 to 5 ounces each. Allow two per serving.

WINGS   Light meat, about 2 ounces each. Allow three to four per serving.

GIBLETS   Gizzard, liver, heart. Boneless and 100 percent meat. Allow 4 ounces per serving.

When cooking chicken for salad or casseroles, count on about 3 cups diced, cooked meat from a 3-pound broiler-fryer.

UNDERSTANDING THE RECIPE ANALYSES

For each recipe in this book, you'll note that we have provided data on the quantities of protein, fat, sodium, carbohydrates, and potassium, as well as the number of calories per serving. If you are on a low-calorie diet or are watching your intake of sodium, for example, these figures should help you gauge your eating habits and help you balance your meals. Bear in mind, however, that the calculations are fundamentally estimates, and are to be followed only in a very general way. The actual quantity of fat, for example, that may be contained in a given portion will vary with how thoroughly you removed fat from the chicken before cooking or with how much care you took in skimming off cooking fat. Likewise, all the figures will vary somewhat depending on how large the portions are that you serve. The analyses are based on the number of portions given as the yield for the recipe.

YIELD

4 servings

Per serving
calories 717, protein 52 g,
fat 30 g, sodium 356 mg,
carbohydrates 58 g,
potassium 608 mg

TIME

20 minutes preparation
1½ hours cooking
10 minutes standing

INGREDIENTS

I chicken (3½ pounds)
2 tablespoons butter or margarine
¼ cup chopped onion
¼ cup chopped celery
½ cup chopped apple
3 cups cooked rice
¼ cup chopped fresh parsley
3 tablespoons raisins
2 dried apricot halves, finely chopped
(about 2 tablespoons)

¼ teaspoon dried thyme
¼ teaspoon salt
⅛ teaspoon dried sage
⅛ teaspoon freshly ground pepper
2 tablespoons apricot jam
I tablespoon orange marmalade

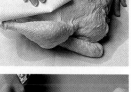

Preheat oven to 375 degrees.

Remove giblets and neck from inside chicken. Rinse chicken, drain well, and pat dry ①.

In large skillet, melt butter over medium heat. Add onion and celery and sauté 5 minutes, or until softened. Remove from heat and stir in apple. Add rice, parsley, raisins, apricots, thyme, salt, sage, and pepper and stir until well mixed. Spoon 2 cups of the stuffing into cavity of chicken ②; do not pack. Place chicken in roasting pan and roast 1 hour, 15 minutes.

During last 5 minutes of chicken cooking time, stir together apricot jam and orange marmalade in a small pan. Cook over low heat, stirring constantly, just until melted. Brush over chicken and roast 15 minutes longer, or until chicken is tender and juices run clear when thigh is pierced ③. Let stand 10 minutes before carving.

To cook extra stuffing, place in a small casserole and cover, or wrap stuffing in aluminum foil. Bake 20 minutes. Remove cover (or open foil) and bake 10 minutes longer.

YIELD

6 servings

Per serving
calories 285, protein 23 g,
fat 13 g, sodium 364 mg,
carbohydrates 18 g,
potassium 206 mg

TIME

15 minutes preparation
35 to 45 minutes cooking

INGREDIENTS

2 tablespoons butter or margarine
3 pounds chicken pieces
2 tablespoons mayonnaise
1 tablespoon spicy brown mustard
1 tablespoon catsup
4 cups bite-size shredded corn cereal,
   crushed

Preheat oven to 400 degrees. While oven is preheating, place butter in a large baking pan and melt in oven.

Remove skin from pieces of chicken ①. In small bowl, stir together mayonnaise, mustard, and catsup, then brush chicken lightly with the mixture. Place crushed cereal on a piece of waxed paper or in a shallow bowl. Roll chicken pieces in crumbs to coat completely ②. Place in a single layer in baking pan ③, turning each piece to coat with butter. Bake until tender, 35 to 45 minutes.

YIELD

6 servings

Per serving
calories 322, protein 39 g,
fat 13 g, sodium 649 mg,
carbohydrates 12 g,
potassium 730 mg

TIME

30 minutes preparation
25 minutes cooking

INGREDIENTS

2 tablespoons vegetable oil
¼ cup chopped onion
1 box (10 ounces) frozen chopped
  spinach, thawed
1 large egg
¼ cup seasoned dry bread crumbs
4 tablespoons freshly grated parmesan
  cheese
1½ teaspoons Dijon-style mustard

3 skinless, boneless whole chicken
  breasts, halved
3 slices (3 to 4 ounces) provolone
  cheese, cut in half
1 box (10 ounces) frozen leaf spinach
1 cup chicken broth
3 tablespoons all-purpose flour
⅛ teaspoon freshly ground pepper

In large skillet, heat 1 tablespoon of the oil over medium heat. Add onion and sauté, stirring occasionally, 5 minutes, or until soft.

Squeeze liquid from chopped spinach ①. Place spinach in a small bowl, along with egg. Using a slotted spoon, remove onion from skillet and add to bowl. Add bread crumbs, 2 tablespoons of the parmesan, and the mustard. Mix until well combined.

Place one chicken-breast half on a flat surface, preferably between two sheets of waxed paper. Using a meat mallet or rolling pin, pound breast to flatten until ¼ inch thick ②. Repeat with remaining breasts.

Place ½ slice provolone on each piece of chicken. Divide spinach mixture among breasts and spread over bottom two thirds of each breast. Starting at a side with spinach, roll up each breast ③; secure with toothpick. Heat remaining 1 tablespoon oil in skillet. Place rolls, seam side up, in skillet; cover and cook over low heat until tender, about 20 minutes.

While chicken is cooking, cook leaf spinach according to package directions. Drain very well and place in an 11 × 7-inch baking dish.

When chicken is tender, remove toothpicks from rolls. Place rolls on top of spinach and keep warm in 200-degree oven.

Preheat broiler.

Stir broth into flour and stir into juices in skillet; add pepper. Bring to a boil, stirring constantly; cook 2 minutes, or until thickened. Pour over chicken and spinach and sprinkle with remaining 2 tablespoons parmesan. Broil 2 minutes, or until lightly browned.

4

YIELD

8 servings

Per serving
calories 635, protein 44 g,
fat 33 g, sodium 888 mg,
carbohydrates 39 g,
potassium 644 mg

TIME

25 minutes preparation
1½ hours baking
10 minutes standing

INGREDIENTS

4 ounces mozzarella cheese, shredded
8 ounces muenster cheese, shredded
1 cup freshly grated parmesan cheese
¼ cup chopped fresh parsley, plus
   additional for garnish
4 tablespoons butter or margarine
1 cup finely chopped onion
½ cup finely chopped celery
¼ cup finely chopped carrot
2 cups (6 ounces) chopped fresh
   mushrooms
⅓ cup all-purpose flour

¼ teaspoon poultry seasoning
½ cup dry white wine
2½ cups chicken broth
1½ cups half-and-half
¼ teaspoon salt
¼ teaspoon freshly ground pepper
4 cups chopped cooked chicken (from
   about one 3½- to 4-pound
   chicken)
12 uncooked lasagne noodles
3 large fresh mushrooms, sliced
Celery leaves (optional)

Mix together the mozzarella, muenster, ½ cup of the parmesan cheese, and ¼ cup parsley; set aside.

In large saucepan, melt butter over medium heat. Add onion, celery, and carrot and sauté, stirring frequently, 10 minutes, or until soft. Stir in chopped mushrooms; sauté 4 to 5 minutes, until soft. Stir in flour and poultry seasoning; cook, stirring, 1 minute. Gradually stir in white wine, then chicken broth and half-and-half. Stir in salt and pepper. Cook sauce, uncovered, over medium-high heat, stirring frequently until it comes to a boil. Boil, uncovered, 2 minutes. Remove from heat and stir in remaining ½ cup parmesan and the chicken.

Preheat oven to 350°F. Spread 1½ cups of the sauce in a 13 × 9-inch baking dish ①. Top with 4 of the uncooked lasagne noodles ②, then top with 1½ cups of the sauce. Sprinkle 1 cup of the cheese mixture on top. Layer 4 more uncooked noodles, 1½ cups of the white sauce, 1 cup cheese mixture, remaining 4 noodles, remaining white sauce, and remaining cheese mixture. Top with sliced mushrooms. Cover with aluminum foil ③ and bake 1 hour 15 minutes. Uncover and bake 15 minutes longer, or until noodles are tender. Sprinkle with chopped parsley; let stand 10 minutes before cutting.

YIELD

4 servings

Per serving
calories 357, protein 33 g,
fat 24 g, sodium 250 mg,
potassium 250 mg

TIME

5 minutes preparation
2 hours marinating
30 to 35 minutes cooking

INGREDIENTS

8 drumsticks (2 pounds)
3 tablespoons olive oil
1 tablespoon lemon juice
1 tablespoon chopped fresh parsley
$\frac{1}{4}$ teaspoon dried rosemary, crushed
$\frac{1}{4}$ teaspoon dried thyme
$\frac{1}{4}$ teaspoon salt
$\frac{1}{8}$ teaspoon dried marjoram

Place drumsticks in a shallow pan. In small bowl, combine olive oil, lemon juice, parsley, rosemary, thyme, salt, and marjoram. Pour over drumsticks. Turn drumsticks to coat in marinade ①. Cover and refrigerate 2 hours, turning drumsticks after 1 hour.

Preheat broiler.

Line a baking sheet with aluminum foil ②. Place drumsticks on foil and spoon half the marinade over them. Broil 7 inches from heat source 20 minutes. Turn drumsticks over and brush with remaining marinade ③. Cook until tender, 10 to 15 minutes longer.

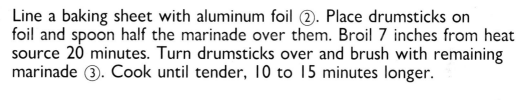

YIELD

6 servings

Per serving
calories 448 g, protein 21g,
fat 31 g, sodium 645 mg,
carbohydrates 21 g,
potassium 367 mg

TIME

15 minutes preparation
20 minutes cooking

INGREDIENTS

1 box (10 ounces) frozen puff pastry
   patty shells
2 tablespoons butter or margarine
1/3 cup chopped onion
1/3 cup sliced celery
1/4 cup diced green bell pepper
1/2 cup sliced fresh mushrooms
1/2 cup (3 ounces) diced cooked ham
2 tablespoons all-purpose flour
1/2 cup chicken broth

2 tablespoons tomato paste
1/2 cup heavy cream
1/8 teaspoon salt
1/8 teaspoon freshly ground pepper
2 cups diced cooked chicken

Bake patty shells according to package directions.

Meanwhile, in medium saucepan, melt 1 tablespoon of the butter over medium heat. Add onion, celery, and green pepper and sauté stirring occasionally, 5 minutes, or until soft. Add mushrooms and ham; sauté 3 minutes. Remove vegetables and ham from saucepan with a slotted spoon ①; set aside.

Melt remaining butter in saucepan. Add flour ② and cook about 1 minute; do not brown. Gradually stir in chicken broth, then tomato paste. Add cream, salt, and pepper and stir until smooth. Stir in chicken and reserved ham and vegetables. Cook until heated through.

Lift off tops of patty shells ③, then remove raw dough from centers. To serve, fill each shell with about 1/2 cup of the chicken and ham mixture; replace tops if desired.

YIELD

4 servings

Per serving
calories 551, protein 34 g,
fat 35 g, sodium 1096 g,
carbohydrates 24 g,
potassium 673 mg

TIME

15 minutes preparation
40 minutes cooking

INGREDIENTS

2 tablespoons vegetable oil
8 chicken thighs (2 pounds)
1½ teaspoons minced garlic
2 large carrots, thinly sliced
1 cup chicken broth
2 tablespoons dry sherry
2 tablespoons honey
1 tablespoon soy sauce
1 tablespoon hoisin sauce
1 teaspoon dry mustard

1 teaspoon minced fresh ginger
½ teaspoon salt
¼ teaspoon freshly ground pepper
2 tablespoons cornstarch
6 ounces fresh snow peas, trimmed, or
   1 package (6 ounces) frozen snow
   peas, thawed
3 small scallions (green and white
   part), trimmed and cut into 1-inch
   pieces

In large skillet, heat oil over high heat. Add thighs and brown on all sides ①. Add garlic; cook 1 minute. Reduce heat to low, cover, and cook 15 minutes.

Uncover skillet and add carrots; cover again and cook 10 minutes. Meanwhile, in small bowl, combine chicken broth, sherry, honey, soy sauce, hoisin sauce, mustard, ginger, salt, and pepper. Stir until combined, then stir in cornstarch ②.

Add snow peas and scallions to skillet. Cook over high heat 3 minutes. Stir sauce, add to skillet ③, and cook, stirring, until sauce is thickened, 2 to 3 minutes.

YIELD

4 servings

Per serving
calories 527, protein 44 g,
fat 32 g, sodium 682 mg,
carbohydrates 15 g,
potassium 629 mg

TIME

20 minutes preparation
45 to 50 minutes cooking

INGREDIENTS

1 chicken (3 pounds), cut into pieces
3 tablespoons all-purpose flour
2 tablespoons olive oil
1 cup chopped onion
4 ounces fresh mushrooms, sliced
1 clove garlic, minced
1/4 cup dry vermouth
1 bay leaf
1 teaspoon granulated sugar
1/2 teaspoon dried oregano

1/2 teaspoon dried basil
1/2 teaspoon salt
1/4 teaspoon dried thyme
1/4 teaspoon freshly ground pepper
1 jar (6 ounces) marinated artichoke
    hearts, drained
10 small pimiento-stuffed green olives,
    halved
6 pitted jumbo ripe olives, sliced

Coat chicken lightly with flour ①. In Dutch oven or large saucepan, heat oil over medium-high heat. Add chicken, a few pieces at a time, and brown on all sides. Remove to plate.

Reduce heat to medium. Add onion, mushrooms, and garlic ② and sauté, stirring, 3 minutes. Stir in vermouth, bay leaf, sugar, oregano, basil, salt, thyme, and pepper. Return chicken to pan. Reduce heat to low, cover, and simmer 30 minutes.

Uncover and stir in artichoke hearts and olives. Cover again and cook until chicken is tender, 10 to 15 minutes longer. Uncover, and with slotted spoon remove chicken and vegetables to serving platter. Skim excess oil off top of sauce ③. Bring to a boil and boil, uncovered, about 1 minute, until reduced and slightly thickened. Remove bay leaf and pour sauce over chicken to serve.

YIELD

4 servings

Per serving
calories 295, protein 29 g,
fat 17 g, sodium 191 mg,
carbohydrates 7 g,
potassium 366 mg

TIME

15 minutes preparation
25 to 30 minutes cooking

INGREDIENTS

2 skinless, boneless whole chicken
   breasts, halved
2 tablespoons all-purpose flour
1 tablespoon freshly grated parmesan
   cheese
Freshly ground pepper
2 tablespoons (or as needed)
   vegetable oil
3 tablespoons butter
2 tablespoons dry white wine

1 tablespoon lemon juice
1 tablespoon chopped fresh parsley
1 lemon, sliced

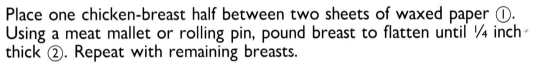

Place one chicken-breast half between two sheets of waxed paper ①. Using a meat mallet or rolling pin, pound breast to flatten until ¼ inch thick ②. Repeat with remaining breasts.

Mix flour, parmesan cheese, and a pinch of pepper. Coat chicken breasts evenly with flour mixture ③.

In large skillet, heat 2 tablespoons oil over medium-high heat. Brown breasts, two halves at a time, on both sides, adding more oil if necessary. Remove browned chicken to plate. Melt butter in same skillet over low heat. Add wine, lemon juice, and parsley, stirring and scraping to dislodge browned bits from bottom of skillet. Return all the breasts to skillet and cook, uncovered, until tender, 3 to 4 minutes per side. Garnish with sliced lemon to serve.

YIELD

6 servings

Per serving
calories 531, protein 25 g,
fat 31 g, sodium 967 mg,
carbohydrates 38 g,
potassium 676 mg

TIME

30 to 35 minutes
preparation
20 minutes cooling
40 minutes cooking

INGREDIENTS

2 cups diced pared all-purpose
    potatoes
1 1/2 cups cut green beans
1 cup diced pared turnip
1/2 cup chopped onion
2 cups chicken broth
1/2 cup all-purpose flour
1 cup heavy cream
1 teaspoon salt
1/4 teaspoon freshly ground pepper

1/8 teaspoon dried rosemary, crushed
1 sheet (half a 17 1/4-ounce package)
    frozen puff pastry, thawed
    according to package directions
2 1/2 cups diced cooked chicken
1 jar (2.5 ounces drained weight)
    sliced mushrooms, drained
2 tablespoons chopped fresh parsley

Place potatoes, green beans, turnip, and onion in large skillet. Pour
1 cup of the chicken broth over vegetables. Bring to simmer, then cover
and cook over low heat, stirring occasionally, until vegetables are just
tender, 10 to 15 minutes. Remove cover and cook until half the liquid has
evaporated.

While vegetables are cooking, stir 1/4 cup of the remaining chicken broth
into flour in small bowl. Stir in remaining 3/4 cup chicken broth and the
cream. Add to skillet along with salt, pepper, and rosemary. Cook, stirring
constantly, over medium heat until thickened. Remove from heat; cool to
room temperature, stirring occasionally to speed cooling.

Meanwhile, preheat oven to 400 degrees.

Unfold pastry ① and flour lightly. Cut four 9 1/2 × 1-inch strips from
pastry ② and set aside. Roll remaining piece until 11 1/2 inches long ③. Cut
off four 11 1/2 × 1-inch strips, setting aside any leftover pastry for another
use.

Stir chicken, mushrooms, and parsley into cooled vegetable mixture. Place
chicken mixture in an 11 × 7-inch (2-quart) baking dish. Place pastry strips,
lattice fashion, over chicken mixture, letting edges hang over edge of dish.
Bake 40 minutes, or until pastry is browned and puffed. Trim any edges off
pastry before serving.

YIELD

6 servings

Per serving
calories 405, protein 23 g,
fat 18 g, sodium 928 mg,
carbohydrates 37 g,
potassium 367 mg

TIME

15 minutes preparation
20 minutes cooking

BISCUITS

1½ cups all-purpose flour
2½ teaspoons baking powder
½ teaspoon salt
3 tablespoons butter or margarine
½ cup milk

CREAMED CHICKEN

3 tablespoons butter or margarine
¼ cup all-purpose flour
1 cup chicken broth
1 cup milk
½ teaspoon salt
⅛ teaspoon freshly ground pepper
⅛ teaspoon dried tarragon
2 cups diced cooked chicken
1 package (10 ounces) frozen peas,
    thawed
3 tablespoons chopped pimiento

Preheat oven to 450 degrees.

To make biscuits, stir together flour, baking powder, and salt in a bowl. Cut in butter until mixture resembles crumbs ①. Add milk and stir until mixture leaves side of bowl ②. Turn dough onto lightly floured board and knead lightly about 10 times. Transfer to a baking sheet and roll into a 9 × 6-inch rectangle. Cut into six 3-inch square biscuits ③. Separate biscuits and bake 12 to 15 minutes.

While biscuits are baking, prepare chicken. In medium saucepan, melt butter over low heat. Stir in flour and cook 1 to 2 minutes; do not brown. Remove from heat and gradually stir in chicken broth and milk. Add salt, pepper, and tarragon. Cook over medium heat until mixture comes to a boil. Cook, uncovered, 1 minute, or until thickened. Stir in chicken, peas, and pimiento. Cook until heated through, 2 to 3 minutes. Serve over biscuits.

12

YIELD

6 servings

Per serving
calories 476, protein 30 g,
fat 24 g, sodium 787 mg,
carbohydrates 32 g,
potassium 302 mg

TIME

25 minutes preparation
40 minutes cooking
10 minutes standing

INGREDIENTS

8 corn tortillas
1 cup sour cream
2 teaspoons ground cumin
1½ teaspoons chili powder
½ teaspoon salt
½ cup sliced scallion (green and
   white parts)
3 cups diced cooked chicken
1 jar (12 ounces) mild taco salsa
1½ cups shredded cheddar cheese

½ small fresh ripe avocado, peeled,
   pitted, and sliced
¼ cup pitted ripe olives, sliced

Preheat oven to 375 degrees.

In small skillet, heat tortillas, one at a time, over low heat until softened, about 30 seconds per side. Set aside.

In large bowl, combine sour cream, cumin, chili powder, and salt; stir until well blended. Stir in scallion and chicken.

Spread ½ cup of the taco salsa into the bottom of an 11 × 7-inch baking dish. Cut 2 tortillas into quarters ①. Using 4 quarters of one tortilla, place the point of each quarter into each of the corners of the baking dish ②. Layer 3 more whole tortillas in dish. Spread half the chicken mixture over the tortillas. Spoon ½ cup of the taco salsa over chicken ③; sprinkle with ¾ cup of the cheese. Layer remaining tortillas as before. Top with remaining chicken mixture and taco salsa. Cover and bake 20 minutes. Remove cover, sprinkle with remaining ¾ cup cheese, and bake 20 minutes longer. Let stand 10 minutes before cutting. Garnish with avocado slices and olives.

YIELD

8 servings

Per serving
calories 399, protein 34 g,
fat 22 g, sodium 298 mg,
carbohydrates 15 g,
potassium 643 mg

TIME

25 minutes preparation
45 minutes cooking

INGREDIENTS

$\frac{1}{2}$ cup all-purpose flour
$\frac{1}{4}$ teaspoon salt
$\frac{1}{4}$ teaspoon freshly ground pepper
$4\frac{1}{2}$ pounds chicken pieces
2 tablespoons (or as needed) olive oil
1 cup chopped onion
8 ounces fresh mushrooms, sliced
1 clove garlic, minced
1 can (28 ounces) crushed, peeled
    tomatoes in purée

$\frac{1}{2}$ cup dry red wine
1 teaspoon granulated sugar
$\frac{1}{4}$ teaspoon dried oregano
$\frac{1}{4}$ teaspoon dried basil
1 bay leaf

In glass pie plate or shallow bowl, stir together flour, salt, and pepper. Coat chicken parts evenly with flour mixture ①.

In large saucepan, heat 2 tablespoons oil over medium-high heat. Add chicken pieces ②, a few at a time, and brown on all sides, adding more oil as necessary; remove browned chicken to plate.

Add onion, mushrooms, and garlic to saucepan ③. Sauté, stirring frequently over medium heat 5 minutes, or until soft. Stir in remaining ingredients and bring to a boil. Return chicken to saucepan, cover, and simmer over low heat 30 minutes. Remove cover and cook 15 minutes longer, or until chicken is tender. Remove chicken to serving platter. Skim fat from surface of sauce and pour sauce over chicken.

YIELD

8 servings

Per serving
calories 319, protein 22 g,
fat 22 g, sodium 357 mg,
carbohydrates 9 g,
potassium 280 mg

TIME

25 minutes preparation
25 minutes cooking

CRÊPES

1 tablespoon butter or margarine
½ cup sliced leek
½ cup chopped fresh mushrooms
¼ cup chopped celery
3 cups diced cooked chicken
⅓ cup mayonnaise
¼ teaspoon salt
¼ teaspoon freshly ground pepper
8 crêpes

SAUCE

3 tablespoons butter or margarine
3 tablespoons all-purpose flour
⅔ cup chicken broth
¼ cup dry white wine
2 tablespoons half-and-half
¾ cup shredded gruyère cheese

To make filling for crêpes, melt butter in large skillet over medium heat. Add leek, mushrooms, and celery and sauté, stirring occasionally, 5 minutes, or until soft. Remove from heat and stir in chicken, mayonnaise, salt, and pepper.

Place ⅓ cup of the chicken filling down center of each crepe ①. Fold sides over filling ② and place crêpes, seam sides down, in an 11 × 7-inch baking pan ③.

Preheat oven to 375 degrees.

To make sauce, melt butter in medium saucepan over low heat. Stir in flour and cook 2 minutes; do not brown. Remove from heat and gradually stir in chicken broth and wine. Return to heat and bring mixture to a boil, stirring constantly. Boil 1 minute, or until thickened. Remove from heat and stir in half-and-half and ½ cup of the cheese. Pour sauce over crêpes in pan. Sprinkle with remaining ¼ cup of the cheese. Bake 25 minutes, or until heated through.

YIELD

6 servings

Per serving
calories 363, protein 29 g,
fat 25 g, sodium 293 mg,
carbohydrates 7 g,
potassium 370 mg

TIME

10 minutes preparation
1 hour chilling

INGREDIENTS

½ cup mayonnaise
1 tablespoon milk
1 tablespoon lemon juice
1 teaspoon curry powder
¼ teaspoon salt
Dash of ground red pepper
4 cups diced cooked chicken
½ cup finely chopped celery
⅓ cup finely chopped onion
¼ cup slivered blanched almonds
3 tablespoons raisins
Lettuce

In medium bowl, combine mayonnaise, milk, lemon juice, curry powder, salt, and red pepper ①. Stir until smooth. Add chicken, celery, onion, almonds, and raisins ②. Stir until all ingredients are coated with dressing ③. Cover and refrigerate at least 1 hour, or until serving time. Serve on a bed of lettuce, accompanied by chutney, if desired.

YIELD

6 servings

Per serving
calories 321, protein 32 g,
fat 11 g, sodium 576 mg,
carbohydrates 24 g,
potassium 952 mg

TIME

15 minutes preparation
55 to 60 minutes cooking

INGREDIENTS

1½ pounds skinless, boneless chicken
   (from about one 3-pound chicken)
2 tablespoons vegetable oil
1 cup chopped onion
1 green bell pepper, seeded and
   chopped
2 tablespoons chili powder
1 teaspoon ground cumin
1 teaspoon dried oregano
1½ teaspoons minced garlic

1 can (16 ounces) peeled tomatoes,
   undrained
3 tablespoons tomato paste
1 can (4 ounces) chopped green
   chilies, drained
1 can (16 ounces) kidney beans,
   drained
⅓ cup shredded cheddar or monterey
   jack cheese

Cut chicken into ¾-inch pieces ①. In large saucepan, heat oil over medium heat. Add chicken and brown on all sides; remove browned chicken to a plate. Add onion and green pepper to saucepan and sauté, stirring occasionally, until soft, 5 to 8 minutes.

Stir in chili powder, cumin, oregano, and garlic. Cook 1 minute. Add tomatoes with juice, tomato paste, and green chilies. With a fork, stir mixture to break tomatoes up ②. Add kidney beans ③ and simmer over low heat 20 minutes.

Stir chicken back into saucepan. Cover and cook, stirring occasionally, 10 minutes. Remove cover and cook 5 minutes longer, or until chicken is tender. Serve topped with shredded cheese.

YIELD

6 servings

Per serving
calories 353, protein 22 g,
fat 13 g, sodium 513 mg,
carbohydrates 35 g,
potassium 541 mg

TIME

20 minutes preparation
25 minutes cooking

INGREDIENTS

1¼ pounds chicken livers
1 tablespoon vegetable oil
3 slices bacon, cut into pieces
1 medium zucchini, sliced
½ cup chopped onion
1 cup long-grain rice
1 can (16 ounces) peeled tomatoes,
　undrained
1¼ cups chicken broth
½ teaspoon Worcestershire sauce

¼ teaspoon dried basil
¼ teaspoon salt
3 drops hot red pepper sauce

Trim chicken livers of any membranes ①. In large skillet, heat oil over medium heat. Add bacon and sauté until browned. Stir in chicken livers and sauté, stirring frequently, over medium-high heat until browned, about 5 minutes. Remove chicken livers and bacon with slotted spoon to plate ②; set aside.

Add zucchini and onion to skillet and sauté 3 minutes. Stir in rice; sauté 1 minute. Drain liquid from tomatoes into a measuring cup ③. If necessary, add enough water to equal ½ cup. Add tomatoes and juice to skillet, stirring to break tomatoes up. Stir in chicken broth, Worcestershire sauce, basil, salt, and hot red pepper sauce. Return chicken livers and bacon to skillet. Bring to a boil. Cover and cook over low heat 20 minutes, uncovering occasionally to stir. Remove cover and cook 5 minutes longer, or until liquid is absorbed and rice is tender.

YIELD

6 servings

Per serving
calories 267, protein 15 g,
fat 16 g, sodium 325 mg,
carbohydrates 16 g,
potassium 374 mg

TIME

25 minutes preparation

INGREDIENTS

1 small Belgian endive
1 small head romaine lettuce
9 anchovies
¼ cup olive oil
1 egg
1 tablespoon lemon juice
¼ cup freshly grated parmesan
   cheese
¼ teaspoon dry mustard
Freshly ground pepper

6 ounces cooked chicken, cut into
   bite-size pieces
½ cup garlic croutons

Cut off root end of endive ①; remove any wilted outer leaves. Wash endive and romaine lettuce. Dry thoroughly on paper towels. Break into bite-size pieces ②.

Finely chop 3 of the anchovies ③. In large bowl, stir together chopped anchovies, olive oil, egg, lemon juice, parmesan, mustard, and a pinch of pepper. With fork, beat until combined. Add romaine and endive and toss until coated with dressing. Add chicken and toss. Garnish with croutons and remaining anchovies.

YIELD

10 servings

Per serving
calories 162, protein 9 g,
fat 12 g, sodium 199 mg,
carbohydrates 3 g,
potassium 134 mg

TIME

15 minutes preparation
15 minutes cooking
8 hours chilling

INGREDIENTS

8 tablespoons butter
1 pound chicken livers, trimmed
1/3 cup chopped onion
1/2 clove garlic, minced
2 tablespoons cognac
1 1/2 ounces cream cheese, softened
1/4 teaspoon salt
1/4 teaspoon freshly ground pepper
1 small red onion, coarsely chopped

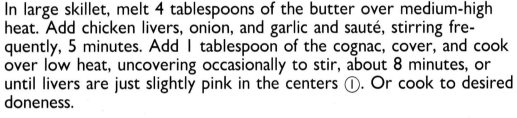

In large skillet, melt 4 tablespoons of the butter over medium-high heat. Add chicken livers, onion, and garlic and sauté, stirring frequently, 5 minutes. Add 1 tablespoon of the cognac, cover, and cook over low heat, uncovering occasionally to stir, about 8 minutes, or until livers are just slightly pink in the centers ①. Or cook to desired doneness.

Transfer mixture to blender container and blend, stopping to scrape down sides of container with rubber scraper ②, until smooth. Add remaining 4 tablespoons butter, 2 tablespoons at a time, blending until smooth. Add cream cheese, remaining 1 tablespoon cognac, salt, and pepper and blend, stopping blender to scrape sides if necessary. Spoon into small bowl or crock ③, cover, and refrigerate at least 8 hours. Serve sprinkled with the red onion, and with crackers.

YIELD

4 servings

Per serving
calories 649, protein 49 g,
fat 42 g, sodium 460 mg,
carbohydrates 16 g,
potassium 1008 mg

TIME

30 minutes preparation
50 minutes to 1 hour
5 minutes cooking

INGREDIENTS

¼ cup all-purpose flour
½ teaspoon freshly ground pepper
1 chicken (3 pounds), cut into 8
   pieces
2 slices bacon, cut into pieces
12 pearl onions, peeled, or 1 large
   white onion, cut into chunks
12 large fresh mushrooms, sliced
1 tablespoon olive oil (optional)
1 cup dry red wine
1 cup chicken broth

½ stalk celery
1 bay leaf
¼ teaspoon dried thyme
1 clove garlic, minced
2 tablespoons chopped fresh parsley

In glass pie plate or shallow bowl, stir together flour and pepper. Coat chicken pieces evenly with flour mixture.

In Dutch oven or large saucepan, fry bacon over medium heat until browned. Remove bacon with slotted spoon to plate. Add onions and mushrooms to drippings in saucepan ① and sauté, stirring occasionally, until soft, about 7 minutes. Remove from pan with slotted spoon and add to bacon. Add chicken to saucepan and sauté until evenly browned on all sides ②, adding 1 tablespoon oil to pan if necessary to prevent chicken from sticking. Return bacon, onions, and mushrooms to pan ③, along with all remaining ingredients except chopped parsley. Cover and simmer until chicken is tender, 45 minutes to 1 hour.

Remove chicken to platter or serving dish. Skim fat from surface of sauce and bring sauce to a boil. Cook, uncovered, until reduced and thickened, about 3 minutes. Remove celery and bay leaf. Pour sauce over chicken. Sprinkle with chopped parsley to serve.

CHICKEN AND POTATO SOUP

RECIPE

21

YIELD

8 servings

Per serving
calories 570, protein 35 g,
fat 32 g, sodium 920 mg,
carbohydrates 36 g,
potassium 937 mg

TIME

20 minutes preparation
55 minutes cooking

INGREDIENTS

1 tablespoon butter or margarine
2 large leeks, thoroughly cleaned and
   sliced
1 cup chopped celery
4 pounds chicken pieces
2 cups chicken broth
1 pound all-purpose potatoes, pared
   and cubed
1 sweet potato (8 ounces) pared and
   cubed

1½ teaspoons salt
¼ teaspoon freshly ground pepper
1 cup milk
½ cup heavy cream
1 can (17 ounces) cream-style corn
Celery leaves (optional)

In a large saucepan, melt butter over medium heat. Add leeks and celery and sauté, stirring occasionally, 10 minutes.

Add chicken pieces, chicken broth, potatoes, sweet potato, salt, and pepper. Cover and simmer 40 minutes, or until chicken is tender.

Remove chicken and set aside (see note). Place one third of the soup in container of food processor or blender ①. Cover and process 1 to 2 minutes, until smooth; remove to bowl. Process remaining soup in two batches. Return all soup to saucepan. Stir in milk, cream, and corn ②. Return chicken pieces to pan and cook until heated through. Garnish with celery leaves if desired.

Note: *Meat may be removed from bones at this point if desired* ③

OVER-BARBECUED CHICKEN

YIELD

8 servings

Per serving
calories 406, protein 41 g,
fat 20 g, sodium 240 mg,
carbohydrates 12 g,
potassium 390 mg

TIME

20 minutes preparation
40 to 50 minutes cooking

INGREDIENTS

1/4 cup red currant jelly
1/4 cup bottled chili sauce
2 tablespoons cider vinegar
2 tablespoons firmly packed brown
   sugar
1 small clove garlic, minced
2 drops hot red pepper sauce
2 chickens (3 pounds each), quartered
Orange slices (optional)

Preheat oven to 375 degrees.

In a small saucepan, stir together jelly, chili sauce, vinegar, sugar, garlic, and red pepper sauce. Set over low heat, stirring occasionally to blend ingredients, then bring to a boil. Reduce heat and simmer 15 minutes, or until sauce is thick and reduced to about 1/3 to 1/2 cup. Remove from heat.

While sauce is cooking, line a baking sheet with aluminum foil ①. Place chicken quarters on baking sheet ②. Bake 15 minutes. Remove from oven and brush chicken with half the sauce ③. Return to oven and bake 15 minutes longer. Brush with remaining sauce and bake 5 to 10 minutes longer, or until chicken is tender. Increase heat to 450 degrees and bake chicken 5 to 7 minutes until glaze is bubbly and lightly browned. Serve garnished with orange slices if desired.

YIELD

6 servings

Per serving
calories 368, protein 20 g,
fat 17 g, sodium 129 mg,
carbohydrates 33 g,
potassium 389 mg

TIME

15 minutes preparation
15 minutes cooking

INGREDIENTS

8 ounces linguine
2 tablespoons vegetable oil
I large clove garlic, minced
12 ounces skinless, boneless chicken,
    cut into pieces
I medium onion, chopped
¼ cup olive oil
I medium zucchini, sliced
I medium yellow squash, sliced
I tomato, chopped
⅓ cup freshly grated parmesan
    cheese

Cook linguine according to package directions ①.

Meanwhile, in a large saucepan, heat vegetable oil and garlic over medium-high heat. Add chicken and onion and sauté, stirring constantly, 5 minutes. Add olive oil, zucchini, and yellow squash ②. Cover and cook over low heat, uncovering occasionally to stir, 10 minutes or until chicken is tender and vegetables are crisp tender.

Drain linguine and stir into mixture in saucepan ③. Garnish with tomato and serve with parmesan.

YIELD

4 servings

Per serving
calories 368, protein 36 g,
fat 18 g, sodium 929 mg,
carbohydrates 19 g,
potassium 859 mg

TIME

20 minutes preparation
15 to 20 minutes cooking

INGREDIENTS

2 skinless, boneless chicken breasts
2 tablespoons soy sauce
1 teaspoon granulated sugar
1 small clove garlic, minced
¾ cup chicken broth
4 teaspoons cornstarch
3 tablespoons peanut oil
4 cups broccoli flowerets and pieces
1 small red bell pepper, seeded and
    cut into strips
1 medium onion, cut into chunks
⅓ cup cashews

Cut chicken into 1-inch strips. In medium bowl, combine soy sauce, sugar, and garlic. Add chicken pieces to bowl and toss to coat with mixture ①. Stir chicken broth into cornstarch in separate bowl and set aside.

Heat 2 tablespoons of the oil in a wok. Add broccoli and red pepper strips. Stir-fry 3 minutes ②. Add onion and stir-fry 3 minutes. Add remaining 1 tablespoon oil, then add chicken with soy sauce and stir-fry 7 to 10 minutes, or until chicken is tender and fully cooked. Stir broth-cornstarch mixture and add to skillet ③. Cook, stirring, 1 to 2 minutes, or until thickened. Stir in cashews and serve.

YIELD

4 servings

Per serving
calories 771, protein 38 g,
fat 60 g, sodium 923 mg,
carbohydrates 19 g,
potassium 939 mg

TIME

15 minutes preparation
45 to 50 minutes cooking

INGREDIENTS

1 pound Italian sweet sausages
2 tablespoons vegetable oil
4 chicken thighs (about 1 1/4 pounds)
1/4 cup water
1 medium onion, sliced
3 medium red new potatoes, pared or
    not, cut into 1-inch chunks
    (2 to 2 1/2 cups)
1 red bell pepper, seeded and cut into
    strips

Cut sausage links into 1 1/2-inch pieces ①. In large skillet, heat oil over medium-high heat. Add sausages and brown on all sides. Add thighs and brown on all sides. Remove skillet from heat and stir in water ②, scraping to dislodge browned bits from bottom of skillet ③. Add onion and potatoes. Cover and cook over low heat, stirring occasionally, until thighs are cooked and potatoes are tender, 35 to 40 minutes.

Remove cover and add red pepper. Cook, uncovered, over medium heat, stirring occasionally but being careful not to break up potatoes, until liquid has evaporated and potatoes and thighs are browned.

CHICKEN TERIYAKI SALAD

YIELD

6 servings

Per serving
calories 422, protein 29 g,
fat 13 g, sodium 1250 mg,
carbohydrates 44 g,
potassium 640 mg

TIME

30 minutes preparation
1 hour marinating
15 minutes cooking
5 minutes cooling

INGREDIENTS

⅓ cup soy sauce
⅓ cup dry sherry
¼ cup firmly packed brown sugar
1 teaspoon dry mustard
1 teaspoon sesame oil
1 teaspoon grated fresh ginger
1 clove garlic, minced
1¼ pounds skinless, boneless chicken
   breasts
8 ounces capellini (extra-thin
   spaghetti)

¼ cup vegetable oil
4 cups shredded Chinese
1 green bell pepper, see
   sliced
½ cup sliced water ches
2 scallions (green and w
   trimmed and cut into
1 tablespoon sesame see

In medium bowl, stir together soy sauce, she
tard, sesame oil, ginger, and garlic. Cut chick
strips ①. Stir into soy mixture. Cover and re

Cook pasta according to package directions,
while, in large skillet, heat vegetable oil over
Drain chicken, reserving marinade. Stir-fry ch
until tender and cooked through. Reduce hea
nade ② and cook 2 minutes. Remove from h

Drain pasta and run under cold water until c
Drain again, very well, then place in a large b
and sauce and toss pasta to coat. Cool about
occasionally.

Stir in cabbage, green pepper, water chestnut
seeds. Serve immediately, or cover and chill u

YIELD

4 servings

Per serving
calories 664, protein 48 g,
fat 42 g, sodium 456 mg,
carbohydrates 23 g,
potassium 1156 mg

TIME

25 minutes preparation
50 minutes cooking

INGREDIENTS

2 tablespoons all-purpose flour
3 pounds chicken pieces
2 tablespoons olive oil
1 cup chopped onion
1 cup sliced fresh mushrooms
1 green bell pepper, seeded and sliced
3 large tomatoes (1 1/4 pounds), cored
   and chopped
1 clove garlic, minced

1/4 cup dry white wine
1/2 teaspoon salt
1/2 teaspoon granulated sugar
1 bay leaf
1/4 teaspoon dried thyme
1/8 teaspoon (or more to taste) ground
   red pepper
1 package (10 ounces) frozen cut
   okra, thawed

Place flour on a sheet of waxed paper or in a shallow bowl. Coat chicken pieces evenly with flour.

In a large skillet, heat olive oil over medium-high heat. Add chicken, a few pieces at a time, and brown on all sides ①; remove browned chicken to plate. Add onion, mushrooms, and green pepper to skillet ② and sauté, stirring frequently, 3 minutes. Stir in tomatoes, garlic, and white wine ③. Cook, stirring frequently, 2 minutes. Stir in salt, sugar, bay leaf, thyme, and ground red pepper. Return chicken to skillet. Cover and cook over low heat, stirring occasionally, 45 minutes, or until chicken is tender. Add okra and cook 5 minutes. Remove bay leaf before serving.

YIELD

10 servings

Per serving
calories 624, protein 30 g,
fat 21 g, sodium 259 mg,
carbohydrates 81 g,
potassium 928 mg

TIME

20 minutes preparation
30 minutes cooking

INGREDIENTS

30 chicken wings
2 teaspoons vegetable oil
1 clove garlic, minced
1 teaspoon minced fresh ginger
1 can (5½ ounces) apricot nectar
2 tablespoons white vinegar
2 tablespoons firmly packed brown
  sugar
1 tablespoon soy sauce
2 tablespoons sweet pickle relish

Ground red pepper
2 green bell peppers, seeded and cut
  into chunks
1 cup orange juice
2 tablespoons cornstarch
2 tomatoes, cut into chunks

Preheat broiler.

Place wings on large baking sheet lined with aluminum foil. Broil about 4 inches from heat source 15 minutes.

While wings are cooking, heat oil in medium saucepan over medium heat. Add garlic and ginger and sauté 1 minute, stirring constantly. Add apricot nectar, vinegar, brown sugar, soy sauce, relish, and a pinch of red pepper to saucepan. Cook, uncovered, stirring occasionally, over medium heat 5 minutes.

After 15 minutes, turn chicken wings over and add green peppers to baking sheet ①. Broil 15 minutes longer, or until wings are tender.

When wings are almost ready, stir together orange juice and cornstarch. Add to saucepan ② and cook, stirring constantly, over medium heat, until sauce is thickened; remove from heat.

Place chicken wings, green peppers, and tomatoes in large bowl ③. Add sauce and toss to coat. Serve immediately.

YIELD

8 servings

Per serving
calories 330, protein 16 g,
fat 19 g, sodium 145 mg,
carbohydrates 24 g,
potassium 696 mg

TIME

20 minutes preparation
5 minutes cooking

INGREDIENTS

4 slices bacon
1/2 cup vegetable oil
3 tablespoons red wine vinegar
1 teaspoon dry mustard
1/4 teaspoon granulated sugar
1/4 teaspoon salt
1/4 teaspoon freshly ground pepper
3 cups cubed cooked chicken
2 pounds red new potatoes, pared or
   not, cooked, cooled, and cut into
   chunks

3 cups cooked fresh (or thawed
   frozen) green beans
1/2 cup chopped celery
1/2 cup chopped red onion

In large skillet, fry bacon until crisp ①. Drain on paper towel and set aside.

In large bowl, stir together oil, vinegar, mustard, sugar, salt, and pepper. Add chicken, potatoes, green beans, celery, and onion. Toss ingredients until coated with dressing ②. Break bacon into pieces ③, mix into salad, and serve.

If desired, salad can be made as far as a day ahead and refrigerated until serving time.

INDEX